UNCARVING THE BLOCK

Picnic 1   5/12   Douglas Kinsey 1969

Barry Goldensohn

UNCARVING THE BLOCK

International Standard Book Number 0-915248-19-0

Library of Congress 78-52889

Designed by Jim Dodds
Printed by Northlight Studio Press
All Rights Reserved

Vermont Crossroads Press
Box 30
Waitsfield, Vermont 05673

ACKNOWLEDGEMENTS

Carleton Misc.: Breathing You In
Arion's Dolphin: A Message to the Fish
              Three Ring Circus
Yale Review: For a Dead Girl
              Avoidance of Tragedy
              "The entire congregation..."
Poetry: Morning of Execution
              The Man of Words Encounters...
              Time and the String Quartet...
              Art of the Angler
Ploughshares: Our Other Mind Problem
Miss. Review: To The Author of a Single Poem
Pig Farmer's Almanac: Istanbul
"L": Metaphor as Fact
Our Generation: What *is* the Condition of Music?
Porch: Epithalamium,
              Lovers Frighten Each Other

Frontispiece: *"Picnic I"* by Douglas Kinsey, 1969

TABLE OF CONTENTS

for Mabel Ross

1

"He is a paper dragon. I can reach
through him with an open hand,"
chirped the Soubrette. "When I walk on
I will be a Great Lady." And roared Alazon
"I am tired of being a big red cheese.
I will shuffle on as graceful as a Saint
talking to birds with articulate fingers."

And I, I stare at the back of my hands
which do not move one way or the other.
Try to understand their curious inertia.
They will not take any part. They are not
my hands. I abstain from them.

The actors squirming in their masks,
the locked hands, even in calling out the names
of their lovers in the act of love, call out your name.
Within me and against my bones your bones grate.

2

Within me and against my bones
your bones grate. You own
the parts of me I keep from my own sight.

Like the poem, your formal stance
alone makes its strict demands:
the city burns, your jewels reflect its light.

No! No jewels. The way your head turns,
the steeps your voice falls. I burn.
We're at lunch. It isn't even night.

This confusion has its own form.
I cannot tell what's inside from
what's out. The form, the form alone is right.

The form, the form alone is right.
Like music entering the body, taking it,
I breathe you in, your sweat and hair. Or clear
like water taken with quick tongues that races
cold through the bodies of the wolves.

Or you beneath me turning
with sharp alto cries into
flushed birds rising
through me and around me,

rising like the solo voice above,
free of, the beat, breaking away into
a greater music, rising
like copulating flies in one ball
of yellow light, hovering over spikes
of dry grass, over trees and spires, the point
in the Sun Dance when the Great Spirit breaks
in, then, only the drums and no rules.

Shit, horse shit, goat shit, the head
of the opposition party struggling away from me forever,
three spies locked mouth to ear,
the bees in the mimosa,
perpetually engorged, perpetual gold—
all have become durable goods.

And her, any change in her
was loss of clear skin, of trust, this
is an act against decay, it was no death;
I knew what she would be in ten years
and touched her.

EPITHALAMIUM

for Roger and Dina

Reaching out with those outrageous
long distance calls to anyone close
to say hello, fly in for brandy, movies,
spiced wine by candlelight,
to watch the storm cross the valley
close to you, a face to lean across
the table to, whose skin is here
at your fingertips, or for your hand,
or new woods for all of you to enter
to scout out its clear places
where the deer graze,
reaching out to bring in.

Bringing in, with the piano, hauled
by farm boys, with rugs, pots, soiled
work clothes, red clay on grey,
the wedge of sky between the elm top
and the roof, quartered
by the window, alien proteins,
her hair in your teeth, the bridge
of her nose pressed into your neck,
the curve of her at rest, wholly
within you between sleeping and waking,
that you smile her morning smile
and she stares your stare,
bringing in to keep.

Keeping. You are ashamed to speak of it:
that you would own her the way she
owns you, and would destroy
the winged life to keep that picture of you
in her eyes intact through blinks and sleeps
to death. Speak of it the way
this clay plaque keeps the print of gears,
this grave rubbing keeps
the knight and lady in their formal stance
who are their own background and foreground;
kept the way art includes: the eye
open, the mouth, the hands, open to receive
and give and keep giving.

It begins in danger always, on the wire
the aerialist, with all breath around her
hung, dives and misses, no, catches the thin
bar and begins the slow triumphant arc
over our heads, her heels over her head
in air spread eagled sailing free and coming in
fast with elephants, drums, trumpets entering
lunging and they catch breath again in the dark
back and shouts break — pennants, horns
and whistles, now, ah, the yes-yes clowns
wave and stamp in bloopy shoes and shriek,
howl, whoop and the whole tent balloons
with exploded breath and the aerialist flips
herself neat onto the elephant and marches
out standing, bowing, waving ostrich plumes,
the clowns disappear in giggles, a dog
rackets outside in the rain and you
push me off and close and roll away
keeping secret till you come again.

We have learned a Mandarin language,
an ingrown puzzle binding us
to talk to one another —
the many ones and others — to disengage

with unfixing clarity our actual selves
as figures from their grounds, the sheets
of glass or broad leaves that hold rain
like beads of sweat on the high arched,

double arched, romanesque brow
above your eyelids, half-closed to disarm.
Here is your face in my hands.
The ground, for now, of all figures of you

dancing in this small circle to shifting
rhythms, with abrupt counterturns
to a Renaissance court. And I,
always a something else thereby.

"Dere hart," you say, "how like you this?"
and you are Anne Boleyn, tragic,
for the moment gay, with young
Sir Thomas Wyatt, ironic gentleness

moving a dazed self into your bare all.
A cavalier? No, a stumbling grenadier
too impatient to undress
his favorite camp-girl after a brawl

or his wife, unsafe at home
in coarse cotton, waving fat arms
spilling the wine, cursing! cursing!
That mourning woman of Lorenzo

secure among her signs,
the veil, the empty ring, the lines
of funereal cypress inside the walls
of her dead lord's demesne.

Her mesocosm: manor, pasture, ponds
are a fictional world in which she finds
herself with a real face that exults:
"I know what young women know.

I will survive this sorrow, You will help."
I lay a flat broad hand into
your child's hand and was engulfed
as if I were the child and you

the swallowing father. "How long
have I been here?" asks White-eye
up from his dungeon, dazzled
in the courtyard. "Ten years? Twenty?"

The patient foreboding of the flesh
tells you nothing. You have been here
so long you want to die. The manacles
still bite. Neither of us holds this whip.

We are part of the crowd
that pokes around the market checking teeth,
biceps, hair, and one another
with the natural curiosity of lovers,

slaves, children, to discover
if there is a living thing
in there, moving
the giant figures through their roles.

THE REVOLUTION DECIDES
NOT TO OCCUR

She is so exotic, for relief I stare
out the window at the ocean
growing black. If I looked at her
steadily I would gape like a clown.

Her rapt smile as she plays her hair
before her face suggests some deep
sufficiency of knowledge. It is the queer
knowledge of Narcissus in his half sleep.

The conversation around her flies
swiftly and I notice her attention pass
through her hair to the thighs
that bulge her tenuous dress.

I become aware that she observes
my thighs but finally with boredom
returns to hers. This order preserves
its dreaming equilibrium.

He does not know where the swaying bridge of her
body, to its own time, touches ground again;
not breasts and hair swaying over him in a caress —
her whole self sways, the center of his storm.

She speaks to him in the modulated alto
with which she speaks to the guys at work,
establishing with that measure, her control:
this distance of the body is herself, inviolate.

He rushes her with crackling voice, or bellowing,
galloping across a rocky field, a bull
with banderillos, wild arm sweeps,
pure ram devotion in a leap across a waterfall

smack into her slow time brass pendulation
that drives him back to the first thing he knows,
his father's hands, insistent and mechanical,
that make a rough graph of that sway:

on outline in a strobe of urgent hands
that brand the air with her. It stays.
Why have I contrived this image for you?
These nervous hands shaping nothing out of nothing.

Reader, with this image as a talisman
ward off your love of the cold and happy ones.

10 THE AVOIDANCE OF TRAGEDY
to Hamlet

If we could purge ourselves like that! Separate you
in a first class cabin on a steamer, admire,
at our farewell, the thickness of the shock-proof wire
enforced glass portholes, approve the round view —
though monotonous — and the cabinetry, the respect
for grain and fit, lament the loss of such an art
of fine carpentry, and with these sweet-smart
indirections seal you off to new prospects
in a country where your restless, prying insight
would earn you a great name in Physics. From the dock
we would see you vanish in a line of white smoke
with your high-minded lust for setting old curses right
that will destroy yourself and all of us. We'd thrive.
But only a fool would dream that we could change our lives.

She feels naked in the small room of her clothes,
exposed in them, and wonders if she is dreaming
of power or weakness, the french doors of her grand
house jammed open through which a gale
shoulders aside its rows of paired lights,

followed by the gray faced officers,
polite, arranging everyone in lines,
their uniforms stretched tight across their thighs,
unbending lines across their faces,
charming how they are confused by her!

She projects her hunters coming for her
from this corner, no, from that, armed
with what? and this doorway, tall stair,
no, that alley — figuring the most
effective arms, open arms and sudden conquest

with viva partisans getting the drop
on the whole sleepy pack, hiding
unbreathing in a double wall while she
arranges the bellowing pursuit safely outside.
Meanwhile her roses play at Portugal.

Walking in a restless sleep, the light
streaming from another body, in lines
around its doors, dazzling through its windows,
"I want in. I want that light," she says
who would not be satisfied by less than love.

I

He leans into you, forward in his chair,
his hands hang loosely over his knees.
Look, no hands! Just eyes and a voice
and the flood it releases!

The part you did not want to see,
the bones with their death-smirk, the heart
through which the blood now shakes
mercilessly, everything inside
the tight siding of your skin you hid

and call to now. You want it out
through the usual doors, storm doors
and screens, breaking the legs
and springs of the couch, thundering
out of the house of the body.

II

She is all awkwardness
curtsying and fussing
with the drape of her dress
patting down her hair
smiling stiffly as if she knew
she was out of place here;

say, a country girl with a chicken,
her preposterous token,
waiting for the lord of the estate,
his formidable manner and small change.

Her modesty betrays her.
She is an agent, a major
in the revolution we continue to resist.

At her request at night
in the black river, the underwater
demolition team sinks down
to work on our life.

That is not a dress. It is a gown.
She commands us. Helpless,
she treats us as children: "Close the book.
Everything, even the life of the mind,
must stop now."

The slippage of style is so fast
the mothers of our archaic class
no longer know how to arrange
a marriage for their daughters.
They cast around for advice
and find that no one, no one knows.
The girls have their own unschooled will
and the men of the right families
behave like pigs. What shall they do
with their delightful Kitty? She is in love
with a series of unsuitable men:
a subterranean, a dancing doll,
an organist, a poet and an organ.
Marriage! Marriage! The smart talk
is of divorce. That is the nature
of the new age: wife from husband,
shall from will. There is no change:
the virtuous have all the power
still, the sinners all the grace.

"DIVORCE IS A SIGN OF KNOWLEDGE IN OUR TIME."

WCW

The old slides obligingly away,
a line of ski-troops peeling off downslope
with muffled guns on deadly orders, leaving
me in my bright cabin high and clear
in the sharp resinous woods and air.
Strange children and a smiling wife and lawyer
whisper down the carpet past the portraits
out the high door. The new
minnows in the cold stream between my fingers
that will not close on them, they nibble
on the hairs of my hand their quick kisses.

TIME AND THE STRING QUARTET
    DOMESTICATE EROS

They are tempestuous in white ties,
black suits and gleaming shoes, seated.

And what proceeds from them in C
sharp minor surely is tempestuous.

It subverts all other order. Abandon
is delicious and to such

ecstatic stuff ! It was arranged
to end. We turn, stand, bang

our knees against the seats, fumble
with our coats, remind ourselves

of home, return. We never once
dreamed of real submission, did we?

(3. Expressing identity or equality...*Dos y dos son
quatro,* Two and two are four; *Amar es sufrir,* To love
is to suffer.)—Dictionary entry.

He is the gay lover no one
wants to liberate. Would you
presume to? From the fastness
of his queer outpost against time?

The lovers, always young, ring him;
a ragged march in torn sandals;
and he is full of favors, knives,
a book, new pants, (try them).

Unwithering their new lashes rising
from new cheeks revealing each
time new eyes. He is locked
to his own perpetual youth.

The loved Other seems himself
complete in his own underwear.
But rules prevail—everywhere—
he loses himself in love,

shattering all he guards. Against
time's taking he has no defense.
Their cheeks toughen, they become
bootsoles in bed, against the thigh

and inner arm, bristle.
They will not stay down
nor any remain his own youth
but will explode into a man and other men.

You made your one poem a cage
to hold yourself in, the way
your page holds the poem.

But here you find yourself poised
in water, deceptively
still, everything drifts

away from you and you have
no place to set your feet. What
will you hold to now

moving in slow circles in
that unseen centrifuge to
its stone edge? Only

one who moves within you, half
understood and unpredictable
keeps a balance with

counterturns and cold enraged stands.
I made this poem to hold you
still for a moment,

for myself, to tell you this.

THE MAN OF WORDS ENCOUNTERS
THE CIRCLE OF INFINITE RADIUS
WHOSE CENTER IS EVERYWHERE
 AND WHOSE CIRCUMFERENCE
IS NOWHERE

Whether your woman comes or goes
or stays, whether your children stay,
their unready faces raised
and open to you, and your books with their strength,
hot mouthfuls of words, always new,
concerns now the steady levelling slant
across the paper that lies in black
order between the blue ruled lines.
It never before struck you, did it,
as important. Suddenly it's late.
Squint hard at what is written.
This late it centers all that matters
at every point. The light is stronger
on the flight above. It shakes in your hand
as you rush the falling stairs.

It will dazzle and then fly, or you will,
having seen the angel's eye
half veiled by heavy lids,
staring forward, in the gallery
as you passed and they dimmed the lights,
shooed you out and you climbed
into the bus to the next city,
the tour miserably timed;
the man in the next seat staring
at a Rolls in *Paris Match;* the half
face of a girl reflected in the window,
bored and dull; a cow, a calf;
and you looking back, only
half knowing what you saw. Sequestered,
you thought safely, remotely,
but now you are arrested
by a disciplined, solitary force
from the interior, an eye
shadowed with its knowledge of you.
Do not oversimplify
the flood of what you knew
all along. The dense texture
of the music confuses you;
the eye seen clear now; you still unsure.

Unsafe, I place myself in this design
here behind my two eyes, secured:
How else not obtrude?

You drag away from me, a disconsort
of musicians following, their antique instruments
new minted for your sparse rites.

They tune up now in random discords
for the serenade to raise your new fort.
All this is done indoors,

And you stare only at the floor, your eyelids
lovely as your eyes. Look, the oriental carpet
has an extra fish, half-a-circle.

The bridesmaids and friends are irrepressible,
all leers, bawdy songs and snickers.
No mystery in this dry ritual,

only a man with whom you do not fear
desire, for "by desire is the world revealed,"
you say, not knowing how the world is hidden.

And I, who can neither give you away
nor keep you, hide myself away, with hope
for light and fire behind these closed doors.

TO BE CLEAR

for Thomas Tallis

I have quarreled with you all day
and most of the night, propped
on an elbow in bed, aching
for rest, burning with little time —
your eyes staring at the ceiling
in the dim light from the street
wide with incomprehension
rolling over to my face. They waver
within faint white and fix
seeking me out as I seek
you and the true words for you,
as this motet about the Passion
filters through the walls and floor
with its precise articulation
of ecstasy and false promise
addressed to no one in particular
as herald of a formal purity
to come when we can close our eyes
into a clarifying sleep.

THE FIGURE OF DESIRE

(on a bas relief by Maillol)

They struggle in the stone toward one another
in the figure of youthful flesh, driven
by itself to its true object, which is like itself —
youthful, driven, in permanent arrest:
the high bust, the long muscles stretched over
the graceful armature of ribs,
the daring angle of the hips ready
for their wild swing, fitting,
fitting. And we, love, roughened by fulfillment,
would find our chocky bodies so figured
in this clear light, satires against desire.
Even our faces are seared.
Only in our half opened mouths, in our eyes,
we see the picture of our true bodies as desire,
not in these rags that wear us.

A MESSAGE TO THE FISH

Penetrating, this water moving down
stream, around my feet, around
and through me, cutting away
walls of stone, loose soil and roots,
widening its banks, see it carry
cold from the mountain down
this twisted coil including me.

And this snapshot wading, this design
is a message for the reliable lady
salmon returning to breed and die,
the whale migrating by faint clues,
dallying in undersea caverns,
dissolving into the small things it eats,
for you with almond eyes, steady
under turbulent hair, fixed on me
in this attrition, this cool going.

The full image is in poor light.
The men form a tight group, one row
sits, the rear stands. I can not
see the faces under wide hats.
The only legend is on the brick
and timber of a baroque facade
which tells us little: "Eureka
Playhouse, Nevada, Nineteen four."
These are not players. I move close
and sit off one end. They stay
out of reach. Only details —
untrim gear and skin —
the crushed hat-brim, torn boot,
frayed pocket, a scarred cheek
are all I recognize.
It too is still — the crescent
of your shoulder, the corner
of your eye by moonlight.
From the dark circle of your dress
coiled on the floor your legs rise
a faint white —
this close I see them tremble.

For you the pathologists suspend their customary black humor
and remember they are solitary;
their confident hands hesitate as on their first day
before opening the unbroken
skin down your long midline or probing with a bright scalpel
the tangle of brown hair
for the line of incision: the smoke from the tremolant
electric Stryker-saw
penetrates them as never before. Their silence
is a conspiracy
to deny the unspeakable: "This thing is more, is more…"
is me lying alongside
invisible, my heart, brains, genitals, forever displaced.

When the sheer wall of hair
that made you the city on the rock
turned gray, suddenly, you dyed it.
When your face creased, you strained
art to preserve it.
And the skin that stayed smooth
through three births, puckers;
silk gives way to lace and quilt.
Now your daughters wear
with savage aplomb, your eyes,
cleared, and hair, and turn you away
from your own beauty
and the world it matters in
to the death of love of the body.
I mourn this loss most.

THE MIND FALLS UNCARING
            INTO ITS IMAGE WORLD

The face of the sleeper drops its dull control
and follows with serene absorption
that familiar self as he preserves
his secrets from the Inquisition
despite exhaustion and the threat of torture
in the white room. Later, hiding
in a hedge of Yerba Santa when the hunters
stamp by he lifts his head and sees
the fissured landscape on its scroll below
and reaches out to scoop
the soft haze in his hands, caress
the nubbly trees and feel the sharp hills
scratch his fingertips, and sees a woman
wave her arms and yell to him, leaning too far
out the window of a tall building in a town
and catches her in one cupped hand
as she begins to fall. Sleeper,
it says, this is your gift. You have survived
one more day the slow rolling of the beast,
discontented, massive in his cave,
excluded by your ordinary mind.

They seem like the pious from the old world,
no wavering, just a forward trudge
black broad hats, black coats
sweeping around them, their eyes fixed ahead
past our stares, on course
among our perilous dividing minds
through the door of home and close the door.
Hidden from us their slow hands, their exultation
at the long disrobing search for someone there
moving the skin under the sliding cloth
raising the arm to glow against the light
naked within the habit of passion.

I call your wife a sea
when I dance with her, not
to rush this sharp salt
sweat that whips about her
to your wavering attention,
nor that when you call
she is always there, waiting,
nor the few ways she is predictable
like her smooth lunar regularity,
but rather to what appears
from a great height like a wrinkling sheet
blown in sun and blinding,.
but this close is felt as force
moving in from glancing green to black.

Music as Civic Order

Ringing the tables of the gaudy plaza
with heads together they buzz and they sway over
scores like forsythia in a strong wind.
Waving their arms and their hands
conducting the shapes out of air,
they weave in their frail steel chairs.
                                    Busy.
They will never offend *il Principe;* easy
to govern. The mayor is lazy, the sheriff
rocks his bulk back in his chair.
His raised feet dance in the air,
a coda, a musical close.

Outlaw Music

Well, now that's over, the door
burst in, the wall split through which
the heavy breathers push to fill
the tight house with dancing, drowning
out the music with their feet and belching
from the beer that has only now
stopped flowing from the stones
and the girls forget themselves, skirts
above their breasts as they flash their white
unsunned asses and the house is all meat,
shrieks and hair, bracing body salts
and ecstasy with everything thrown back,
walls and heads, mouths and all throats
pouring full and lost in all that opening.

Every violence, duplicity
or cold twist the mind can give
to instinct is shrined alive
in some quarter of this city.

Bureaucrats, old priests
and police chiefs survive
best its devious elaborations, by
denying everything exists

in a *patois* the guide-books call song
—its ironies are so urbane,
its cadences can so seduce. Down
fall the defenses of the long

time whore, clinched to artifice,
to whom desire is disease;
ah, with quick turning phrase
they violate with openness.

Down the chic dress, the paste
diamond choker, pearls, girdle,
down the garter belt, the gold bird
medallion clangs down, bra and breasts,

and the heart falls open, flesh
locked until trust flashes
for the last time. Whoosh,
the game is over, love. Go home.

This moss is the only pubic mat I wish,
the wife who is fast and cold, seductive bones;
these trees, undermined with their roots in air, the knees
that wrap around me as they wrap the brook, the beams
of a fallen barn I enter. In the stream
awkward crayfish grope about their urgencies
and I exact from under roots and stones
with great deceit the last quick fish.

It springs together; inner
room by room, furnished
and complete, the walls white,
the window full of light,
that chair, that bed, as the eye
and vague self press
through each gate, door
and hall, then the whole city —
an intricate library,
baroque hotels and bars,
bright curving marble
stairs, parabolic
bridges and dark shops
in their shadows, old friends
who will come back
stately in their piled hair
or dragging children behind them
filling the hall steadily
like sand into the bottom
bell of an hourglass.
One loses no one here.
Through a doorway a familiar
arched waist you lean
forward to touch as she speaks
to another across a table;
and you build forever,
fill each room with crowds,
knots and suave compelling
guides in order to discover
yourself at the opera
or loitering in the street.

Everyone is paper
for our moral designs:
"Here, here is the word for you,"

and we write it on them,
like the states and networks
with their vast designs on us.

Let yours dissolve. We don't
need it — just the faces,
the design of living faces, moving

with their own skin and eyes
toward us, curious, hovering,
and eager to speak. "We too

are living," they say. "He
misunderstood, wrote us down as dead,
but brought us here to live, Dante."

That you are sexually aroused by
doctor and dentist
does not cut my ice. I do not tinker
with holy places.

Sing, sing, what shall I sing

I am pleased to arouse the woman I love
with the pleasure
of a fine habit. Like bringing flowers as
a constant surprise.

Your guesses are wild. I am neither fat
nor deceitful, though
it is not for me to tell you so. I
can offer nothing

Do, do, what shall I do

to save a thickening beauty. Are you
there? You have become
an abstraction because you have made a
ludicrous mistake.

With my book by your bed you think you have
me too. There are no
confessions in it. I lay that dead weight
on those who love me

Sing, sing

with whom I am just now in supply.
I made this strange poem
for you. Because it excludes fantasy
you may possess it

Do, do

entirely, unlike any private self,
mine or even yours.

Nothing interests him so much as himself.
Nothing else will drive him to invent
but the need for a world in which he will be the center.
First the canoe close around him
then the bright lake of faces
then the moon, the unclouded face of his father.
Look at him in his windowless apartment
typing while a drunken friend
fills his couch with crab lice
the letter urging him to be a pharmacist
soaks up spilled coffee on the enamel table.
He calls to the dust motes that swirl with him
in the stellar wind and they turn their blank faces:
"Do you see that shining down there? It is me!"

THE MORNING OF EXECUTION

A tree nubile with unripe plums
and a low bush with green hard
lemons shadow the prison yard.
The morning mist has not yet
burned away and on the wires
the dew still shines. The silent visitors
reach small gifts through to me.
I turn from them and care only
for the windfall fruits, redlaced,
green and spotted in the short grass,
becoming soft jewels in the hand.
Cold and puzzled by this waste.

A band, high brass, a faint relentless beat
dividing into random counterpoint
around the Civil War Monument,
approaching, and increasingly distinct,
a full procession chanting, and your office mate
stares at you, turns away, lights a cigarette
and down the straight avenue the band's
sound increases, the crowd runs in advance;
chattering and eyes and the low window;
you deny no longer that you know; the chant
is peaceful this close; a drummer in a campaign hat
wanders away tapping idly; you can
no longer resist moving out into the street
to be in a firmer position to hear the news
they have come to deliver formally: defeat
of your main force, loss of the world and desire,
the cement abrades your knees, you feel it
against your teeth, they lift you as you faint
trying to escape the last words of that choir.

A MAN, A WOMAN, A MALE MIDWIFE

for David Werner

The child lay transverse in the womb, stalled,
its head a knot above the bony hip;
she squatted with her arms across his knees
off the edge of the bed, and he leaned
into her, his face into her neck, their arms
rising, tangled in one another like the bole
of the strangler fig that shades the room —
indistinct their dark limbs together.

I disentangle them and lay her out in bed
where my hands can realign the child
under her dark skirts in a dark room.
Crossed with finger streaks her greased belly shines,
the tracks of small forces pressing for release.

The respirator grunts, insists;
its tube gorges mother's throat;
her eyelids are grained with a fine sweat;
her skin so transparent everywhere

the white skull shines through;
not even her hands recognize
my hands. I ran home. This was the place
I did not hold to till the artery

erratic, a cat under a sheet,
stopped bouncing in her neck.
I ran. So transparent. Everywhere
the white skull shines through.

Clouds of blind children scatter from their bus
down the hillside to the concert on the lower lawn
stumble and grope around an unwavering
central eye, a volunteer who whispers "Stay with me.
Stay close," brings back the break-aways who lurch
into shrubs and low walls, and directs them
in their group course downhill to the music.
Lit sidelong by the late sun
they pass from half-glare to silhouette
disappearing in their shadows — to a place
on the lawn among our outstretched legs
with their shocking faces which they cannot compose.

At the funeral of our closest suicide
our own faces, stained and shapeless,
peer into one another's suddenly exposed
private places in an unlit room as we feel
for what we are not allowed to see.
Now we envy that unwavering central eye
whose "Stay with me. Stay close," we might
during this graceless stumble not replace
with the words that we would use
in a poem about ourselves: clear-eyed, metallic,
withering, imprudent, satiate, letters, suave,
burned letters and celestial distance.

I cannot see the young boy running.
I can hear him. On the low desk
my cheek rests on my fist.
The voice on the telephone is not
my young son returning. It is the ex-
husband of my sister. He will stop by.
I cannot see the young boy running.
I can hear his arms thrown out and back
at his sides, his feet crash, his fight for breath.

D.O.A.

After the heart was shocked, uselessly,
and the monitor showed only the stray
diminishing spasms on its screen, leaving
we covered his chest with the shirt we cut away

and let his heart trickle down in an empty room.
Our frenzy was *pro forma;* he was dead
before he hit the street downtown, too long ago
to be disturbed to new life on this bed.

All his valves were locked on *open wide:*
I turned him over from a puddle of shit
face down into a pool of vomit, when the coroner
arrived to check him out and finish it.

Before his wife came we went back in,
closed up his shirt again, sponged his face
then pulled back the sheet lingeringly for her,
a gentle piece of theatre to embrace

the living with our real care.

With smeared mascara and a dripping nose
her mother follows an aunt around the city
searching, searching, and more remote
than ever her father is just another echo
in the abandoned house, and the rabbi
chided us as wilfully blind
who, when called, slid our spadefuls of dirt
down the side of the grave and did not
dump them on that still resonating box.

One, the first, made clever wooden toys
and touched me warmly and often wildly
which was fortunate for me.

Another, for irreverence, esoteric
learning, poems that kicked down doors
seeking authority; his martyrdom in madness.

Another could whistle entire sonatas,
groaned and twisted his ear as he thought
and had a "passionate devotion to truth."

Another had no use for truth, only
rage against absurd sanity, restraints,
politics, painful urine, stiffening age.

The ideals are all dead, the real
remains for warmth with talk of cars,
the horses, something reliable.

The entire congregation of some exotic sect
of Hasidim takes over the airport; everywhere
black overcoats and bright skullcaps run
for the planes as if the game were over
and the fans rush the heroes on the field.
From each plane many famous rabbis disembark,
a committee of great teachers has arrived
from the air. The disciples circle them
and sing, some throw open their coats
in unthinkable abandon, some even their shirts,
they raise their arms, drumsticks that flap
in black sleeves, and beat against their chests
with a steady tempo forward; one red face
and curly beard flashes against the lattice
of the hangar wall with his mouth locked open.
They hand out bills with pictures of praying Jews.
They march the rabbis out into the night
with Bom, Bu-Bu, Bom-Bom, Bom-Bu-Bu, Bom-Bom, Bom,
the bridegroom's song for the Sabbath Queen arriving.
I do not understand why my cheeks are wet:
surely this must be the millenium.
I lean forward, choked, unable to laugh,
even at myself deceived again
by a brotherhood I stand outside of.
This is the dream from which I wake up crying.

Why do you want to be a rabbi? I ask myself.
The fallen temple is mouldering
and the rabbinate has lost its once high role.
They sing at people. You can't even sing.

The world is in Galut. In disorder
the divine sparks will not be called to
by a chicken. For this doubter
I have an answer: what does the rabbi do,

faced with wild hopes, lunatic messiah,
the dream of love destroyed?
He says, reminding us of our diaspora
what I say to my own heart always

deceived by everything I trust most
in myself: expect nothing!
And the temple, wrecked, rises
to salute truth with a sharp steel wing.

At our most cold and irreverent
when we are gifted with clear sight
we might have glimpsed that he too
was a fool, bare and poor.

But now that she has left him
this is easier to see. He is naked
of all his adornments: father,
house-holder, husband to such a brilliant thing.

In the farthest back row of the *shul*
his mother holds his arm
while he struggles with the second vision
of his life as his face flinches in his hands.

If he is cheered at all
it is by the sight of us, watching her
at once passionate and unearthly —
white veils, musk, silk — as she spins off

dazzling us with her new freedom,
killing the old law with new life.

CUTTING LOSSES

for David Werner

> Let the girl die and Tom, drowned
> batter against the hedge and the deer
> listen to the black water roar
> under the ice in which its head is jammed.

She chases our mules across the square
with a gang of boys: "Mula! Mula!
Vengame! Stupido!" The expense
of her repair will sink the clinic
and its penniless dependents:
the tuberculous, the dysenteric
children, damages of gunshot
and knife, fungus and sun and worms.
The surgery she needs is half
our yearly budget which we beg. We must
stand back from this and let her die. Our love
sinks with her. Lily of the valley,
bellflower, her droopy gaiety survives
on very temporary measures.

> Let the girl die and Tom, drowned
> batter against the hedge and the deer
> listen to the black water roar
> under the ice in which its head is jammed.

From the upper window
in a half circle, we can see him
batter against the hedge of black willows.
His wife whispers and prays between her teeth.
The willows bend and spring back and hold
against the water, too fast to walk in,
swim in. It caught him coming from the barn
and tumbled him, who now is out of reach
in flood. This may go on for days,
compelled to watch him bloat
as the hedge holds and no one
dare move out to him; not his sons,
his wife, his friends, his hired hands,
pressed here in a half circle against
the upper window in flood.

Let the girl die and Tom, drowned
batter against the hedge and the deer
listen to the black water roar
under the ice in which its head is jammed.

They brought it down on the ridge
over the bank. I saw the iced-over
film of blood and a circle of dog tracks
where they started on the ham-strings,
and it was dragged still living
on to the frozen river where they ate
the hindquarters first
and finished him off today, as he melted
overnight a foot deep into snow
before dying with the dogs returning,
welcome at the long curved neck.
When I came on him he was still warm;
the dogs backed off, unsure
whether to go or stay there with me.

Let the girl die and Tom, drowned
batter against the hedge and the deer
listen to the black water roar
under the ice in which its head is jammed.

Andres could not stand back
and carried her when she collapsed
on local busses holding the I.V.
above her swollen brain into Los Angeles
the clinic foundering behind for partial love
in bills, for new donors and money.
Her recovery a poor chance.

The second day we walked out
in a human chain and pulled Tom down
tangled in willows.
The women laid him out in the deep bed
and washed the mud away and left him
hard and white, sinking in coarse blankets,
folded and composed with silver eyes.

I cut a rib roast from the cooling deer
and called together friends
who squander themselves in work as if
there were no other pleasure, to celebrate
in a dumb ceremony that we were still
alive together here, to which we ate.

Add to your catechism under Grace
the perfectly flipped thing, the sudden
appearance of George
the morning after the cat
ate the young rabbit we thought
we saved from her the night before;
she saved for us the paws and ears;
George in a silk bathrobe moving
his glasses around to make sure
he was seeing what he saw
scooped the pieces in a dustpan
leaned out the kitchen window
backward, never looking, never
taking his eyes off me as we talked,
flipped the pieces in a pure
parabolic cluster into
a garbage can, top off,
thirty feet across the yard.
This is the grace of the blind, stumbling:
Hollis tossing me to save me
from the sight of my girl sitting
on her old boyfriend's knee (I
never saw!) out the door, inter-
posing his opaque whimsical self
between me and the amorous
carnage within, into his car
for a top-down, stand-up wild
careen through the college town;
all things, (I never saw!), street
dogs, imperious school crossing guards,
The politic greeting all comers at once
with the same smile North and South, all
in that whirl and spring (I never saw!)
with the sudden appearance of grace.

You are the lowland. All streams
flow to you. Why do you stall me
with slim eurasian androgynes curling
and uncurling, gold silk blowing, on my fenders,
windshield, hood? Why, when my soul would plunge
through traffic do their quick fingers reach
through and tap staccato on my steering
wheel and scare my children with their peeping
tree-frog laughter? They jerk
their heads like electric dolls with short circuits.
They batter up thunder with their toy fists.
I have contracted to come to you in peace
but you gather these forgotten images against me.
I will take them down to you. I will carry them.
I will come on foot.

You are the lowland. All streams
flow to you. I see you from where I am —
I am — standing, urgent, circling around you
circling around me, trying to talk
to you who never talk. How else
find you out?
Like when she left me in the restaurant,
walked out fierce — I was being thick,
swallowed slow and rose to the window.
In the plate glass, the bright room
with all people eating; myself
stopped and clumsy, my shadow
the only dark place to see through.
I saw her figure in the watery street
move into many figures *
moving. You walked behind
and through me. You have not gone. I stand
here talking to you.

54 You are the lowland. With a typed list
of witnesses I set out for you.
Eight pages in a packet, waterproof.
I will follow the large streams down
this spring thaw as they join
one another in their narrow stone beds
gathering to white violence screaming
for the too small passage out to more space
before they enter at last the slow river
that pushes along the valley floor. At the inn
they will file out to greet me. The innkeeper's wife
will bring hot towels and the cook will retreat
to the wall. At the end of my stay I will be so changed
they will shove me off my cot. I will no longer
need the list of witnesses.

You are the lowland. All streams
flow to you. The road down is thick with fathers
yammering in claques, crowding, coming between
us and the clean descent, gristle clogging
the wheels, moaning like 'cellos in the gears.
They want us to be water in the sea of them, lowering
ourselves together into the reservoir
entering together the sun and air. Never
in years do they move, they soak into the roads.
Behind, their bad-tasting, ill-fitting lives
we push into, eating our way through
the live stew of them, following our teeth down
and our waists soften and we join new clubs
and they are twice dead as we begin.

You are the lowland. All streams
flow to you. Your mind flows obscurely; the pike
and crayfish poking at the lotus root,
the catfish and the skittish trout, each
speckled stone, seem in their depths to play
upon its surface in a trick of bent light
or seem like one tesselated thing
seen faintly beneath its black skin.
Among your warm, worn-in shoe of a wife,
the lover that flew off in a cloud of insults
or the girl who climbs all over you in bed,
you can not and will not choose.
Now you can ask of love or stoned fucking:
which sinks deepest in you? Sounding
with both, keeping both within.

You are the lowland. All streams
flow to you. She said, "To me. Yielding
to all like ice melting, descending
the ladder of love to the unloved body moving
within me, quiet, worthless, low, I am
an empty space for all men to live in.
I burned the rich dresses that my father
gave me when I married, even the gold
embroidered silk. I left my husband to curse
in the house and keep it. The maids make faces at him.
I am a town under siege. The men, the pricks,
within me dream of having me in peace,
each one a bully. I am most true
when most open to most men. They must
renounce me as I renounce them."
And I, what could *I* say?

All streams
flow to you. But the wardens of beautiful women
and beautiful men have wired ahead in codes:
we and our wards are circling and circling. Stop.
How do we reach who cannot touch. Yours.
She said: O, mother, father — from Anne a nose,
from Willard his firm chin, from Nona hair —
I dove in, rose too long later, stiff,
doubled in size, leaky, unwieldy as a roped hog.
With Love. Stop. They have their own
silent signals, like *there's one, there's one,*
meaning, not the hunter hot after game
nor the hunted in panic away, but another game
where the slain one scrambles up and keeps on running,
enacted with such calm before us
their keepers in the migrating wildlife preserve. Stop.

You are the lowland. I dreamed of visiting
and wound up talking to your husband
who couldn't even catch my name.
My book swung open, each page
painted over, thick with muddy temperas.
I never wanted such obscene safety.
Our friends have new friends for you
and you relax again and lean
your chair against the wall, hold up
a wine glass and across your face
the slight smile, that even in the half-
light of an empty restaurant
on a waitress stops my throat.
I carry you with me still. You are stuck
here in my throat.

All streams
flow to you. Her tears. Her tears.
And they fuss about her with patient voices.
We cannot have our mothers or fathers
either naked or in their Christmas pajamas.
"And the Bishop, dear, is not for you,"
and there is no comfort for her and brother
and sister pour her more coffee. *A maid refus'd.*
The Archbishop comforts the Bishop
who knows his peace lies in his celibate life
his house that is spacious and light, the garden
with rhododendrons, early and late,
their faint odor as he climbs the stairs
and the organ tone of bees in the bright mimosa.
Rewards chill the service. You are the lowland.
In the tide pools the water eddies
over the rooted things that wave their thousand arms.

You are the lowland. All streams
flow to you. Protect now Alex in the prow
of an Amazon piroque wearing tight yellow
slacks, a silk shirt billowing, Baroque,
waving his cigar, his red hair waving.
He will attract the dart of a savage cadre
with a blowgun who will disengage into a smile
his filed teeth behind the leaves. Curare
will stiffen his mannerist rigor.
Sit him down, at least. Read him Mao,
at least, to recognize a world outside
that sweet, smoky, ornamental head,
that charm. He understands only his own
style of success: women run to him and then
away, like children with a base in tag.

You are the lowland. All streams
flow to you. Disinter this poet
from his stone tomb in the family plot.
Enter and dislodge those poems he could not
bring himself to speak — addressed
to you. Reclaim them. Batter the stiffness
of his male will, his well mannered style.
With your small fingers and your harsh hand
get between his fingers, bend the wrist
forward, break his rigid fist open,
loosen his tongue with your tongue.
He died too young — was born old.
Look at those stiff pathetic gestures,
elbows stuck to his ribs. Look at that walk.

You are the lowland. I play
tough with you, pretending you are weak
and running from your urge to throw yourself
with desperate abandon into me
or any man playing manly.
You hold my arm in this play leaning
into me. Your gravity
is desperation under great restraint.
On my oak arm your hips swing like slack rope.
But this is my play. I play both parts. You
stay shy and smile like an amused infant,
return each marking stone, let the jungle return
and renew your burnt-over garden as you burn
and clear another, let me grow back,
a tree seedling in your swiddening. I will be,
finally, a "mother of gardens."

You are the lowland. All streams　　　　　　　　59
flow to you. But Rich, the lonely bastard,
didn't know he was in line or that there was a line
and when his time was up he didn't know he wasn't ready
and there he was with his pants around his knees
and the light went on spinning and someone whacked him
real hard in the back of the head and roared
and the lady said "You next" and he was so surprised
he reached out to keep from falling down the stairs
and he fell but by the time he was halfway down it didn't matter
and he didn't know if he'd see his parents there
and his kids didn't know beans about the business
and they didn't even have a shroud
and no one knew how to make one.

You are the lowland. So I lay me down
filled up with strychnine to retire
to wanting one thing only, thus
consigned to planning in a rational State,
the quadruped family, the daily grind
and hired heart; stretched
out myself since no sudden breath-
breaking convulsion stretched me,
involuntary torsion cracking bone and
tendon with its going-out-of-place
and woke refreshed.
My daughter and my boss smile over me.
My son and wife are busy in another room.
My friends, my students, mill and grind downstairs.
And I have swallowed something and survived.

60   You are the lowland. All streams
     flow to you. In respect to which the rash
     Sennacherib spoke of Babylon this vaunt:
     The city and its houses, from foundation to tower,
     I destroyed, I devastated, I burned with fire.
     The wall and the outer wall, temples and gods,
     I razed and dumped them into the Arakthu Canal.
     Through the midst of that city I dug channels,
     I flooded its site and made its destruction complete
     for the cool image of the fire on the wide Canal,
     to sail on; to seize a girl on, to feel like god's
     katabolist, possess the girl, sink the hacked body
     in the Canal, scattering the ghost
     out of its hammering channels. No god
     is complete unless his power is complete
     and we cook our own pigs over our own fire.

     You are the lowland. All streams
     flow to you. Seated, according to the Law,
     or standing. Without wine. This is not Eros
     we pray to who would prefer Sennacherib
     and his crazy goyim and their horses.
     We woo you with elbows on a desk
     one leaves for more coffee only; driven
     from gardens and gardens; turning
     spirit into food in circuses; dying
     together in sealed rooms; celebrants
     with tears at the old wall. We civilize
     ourselves to civilize you. Here is your book.
     These are the letters of your name.
     An owlet staring at an owl. Why
     the silence and the carrion stinking breath?

You are the lowland. And I am a scrap
blowing about between friends
down the stairs with Marvin
across the parking lot with Harry Oster
up the hall to Don and back
to something I need to know from Stavros:
all the time watching names change,
sniffing fenceposts, tongue slavering
down, aimless dog, maybe,
but earnest, earnest; protected thereby
from a sedimentary life.
This is the pleasure of the housefly
following his own serious nature, hidden
from us this joy. Nothing has no name.

      All streams
flow to you. Like the roofer moving
so still I did not know that he was human
till he passed across the beam; like the three
retired workingmen in Moline with faces
like radar screens installed over guns watching
the young reporters zip babbling into the *Times
Democrat* as a wedge of clouds passes
across a wet stone, reflected. Checked
unwrinkling shirts stretched down into their vast pants.
They don't move to get where they will go,
where they want to go, into the river of wind
that moves within the susurrating trees,
sunset coming on Stonehenge, breaking red
sidelong on gray, making the stones flesh.

You are the lowland. All streams
flow to you. You hesitate like one
wading in a quick stream, each stone
unsure with wet moss under foot
in the tangling and untangling water.
Tentative, tentative,
your hand is on the door which opens to you,
you are a deer among the flowering
alfalfa, engorged with all that green and yellow,
with those vulnerable eyes alert,
swinging about, alert. All sinew and surprising
softness yielding. And to that courtesy, she yields
letting her robe, her arms long and thin, fall,
an Easter lily falling open. This we call
marching without moving.

     I dream of falling
with breath held to the never arrived at
moving impact point, desparate arms
against air in which I don't fly
dropping from the giant parent,
towering ice-box, skyscraper, down.
Below *you* nothing. No fall is possible
from your low richness, your alluvium,
in which every live thing rots
to richness, greenness, brightlaced,
the music of the duck, cock, squirrel, the scream
of the weasel, bee-hum, the faint curled trail
of crawlers, many dark eyes, my children.
You are the lowland. Tall grass and lines
of silver poplar in the black earth. All streams
flow to you.